THE DOOR IN T

By the same author:

THE DOOR IN
THE WALL

Charles Tomlinson

Oxford   New York

OXFORD UNIVERSITY PRESS

1992

Oxford University Press, Walton Street, Oxford OX2 6DP

Oxford   New York   Toronto
Delhi   Bombay   Calcutta   Madras   Karachi
Petaling Jaya   Singapore   Hong Kong   Tokyo
Nairobi   Dar es Salaam   Cape Town
Melbourne   Auckland
and associated companies in
Berlin   Ibadan

Oxford is a trade mark of Oxford University Press

First published in Oxford Poets
as an Oxford University Press paperback 1992

British Library Cataloguing-in-Publication Data
Data available

Library of Congress Cataloging-in-Publication Data
Tomlinson, Charles, 1927–
The door in the wall / Charles Tomlinson.
p.   cm.—(Oxford poets)
I. Title   II. Series.
PR6039.O349D66   1992   821'.914–dc20   91–45855
ISBN 0–19–282939–4

Typeset by Rowland Phototypesetting Ltd
Bury St Edmunds, Suffolk
Printed in Hong Kong

To Brenda

ACKNOWLEDGEMENTS

Acknowledgements are due to the editors of the following: *Agenda*, Bête Noire, *The Gettysburg Review*, *The Graham House Review*, *Modern Painters*, *The North*, *Northward Journal*, *The Paris Review*, *Ploughshares*, *The Poetry Book Society Anthology*, *Poetry* (Chicago), *Poetry Nation Review*, *Poetry Review*, *Quadrant* (Australia), *Scripsi* (Australia), *The Times Literary Supplement*. The following pieces first appeared in *The Hudson Review*: 'Siena in Sixty-Eight', 'Paris in Sixty-Nine', 'In a Cambridge Garden', 'At Hanratty's', 'Blaubeuren', 'Upstate', 'Picking Mushrooms by Moonlight', 'Response to Hopkins'.

CONTENTS

THE OPERATION

A cold spring morning sees
    The man who has come to trim trees
In the valley wood, up against a sky
    That looks down, through and into
A cat's cradle of twigs and branches.
    The man paces this swaying cage,
Giving thought to the size and shape
    Of what he must do, exploring
Floor by floor each pliant storey
    Threatened by rot and over-crowding:
He weighs by eye what high limbs
    Stand to fall, when winter squalls
Rake the valley, and rounds out
    His loppings to please the tidy mind
Of the owner of these trees. Then
    Into action: standing there
Forks apart, spanning half a branch,
    He power-saws the other half off
And scaling a stair of boughs, repeats
    At each rung his noisy squaring.
But what finesse—raucousness apart
    As the blade combusts—in the way that he
Slices the slender outgrowths from the tree,
    Works at it with a dabbing motion,
Then leans back, inspects and jabs again—
    Painting not pruning: he is as much
Making a tree as taking a tree apart,
    Walking a world of his own creation.
He darts with his saw, having at what he sees
    Like a slightly clumsy fencer. No—
'Clumsy' cannot be just. Who'd dare
    Fence on a beech bough, trust
To sprung pliancy fifty feet and more
    In air? A voice-over—caught
Between bursts from the ignited saw,
    Prompting *More to the right, more*
To the road side—proceeds from the critic
    (The artist heeds him, too) who lies
Stretched across the cab-roof of a truck
    Sizing up the shape of the new
Treescape after the morning's abbreviations:

That'll do. The expert in metamorphoses
Restrains his saw, and leans
    Down into the twiggery to extricate
Boughs that have lodged in there,
    Tosses them to the ground with a crackling roar.
The painter and the fencer now disappear:
    He has one more image to dance
In and out of, and clings to his rope
    As a 'Me Tarzan' swing returns him
To the top of his ladder: he trots down,
    Hopping earthwards from five feet up
And walks horizontally away—primate
    Into man—to put a distance between
Himself and what he has done, and to survey it:
    The hard hat he appeared to be wearing
Turns out to be his own red hair.
    Then the corpse on the cab-roof
Suddenly resurrects: *Not bad*.
    His eyes—he is grounded, too—take in
The fallen logs they must soon begin
    Piling aboard and the litter along the road
To be gathered and fired, before moving on
    Down the freshly tarred approaches. Evening:
And the procession of their fires dies back
    To heaps of glowing ash, and a low haze
Starts climbing throughout the trees,
    Altering, as it flows into the twilight,
The million burin strokes of branches
    To soft charcoal lines, the incense
Leaving the senses open to the night.

THE CLEARANCE

They have fired the brush in the half-felled wood:
    Extinguishing piles still smoke on, blue;
Beacons of briars and ivy blazing through,
    Crest the detritus. A glitter
And, suddenly red, a starburst breaks
    As the wind takes hold, and the burnings
And the glows go spreading uphill
    Into the wood-heart. The cut logs
Tell, in their greenness, of how wet
    The wood was, that now lets in
The hilltop horizon and the sky.
    Fresh plantings will branch out there,
Feel the embrace of entering air—
    Spaced to receive our climbing glance
That can survey all of the falling stream
    Woodland had hidden away, a white
Rope the water lets down
    Sounding closer and closer against the ear,
A keen, clear flight to the feet of whoever is standing here.

SIENA IN SIXTY-EIGHT

The town band, swaying dreamily on its feet,
    Under the portraits of Gramsci and Ho,
Play 'Selections from *Norma*', and the moon,
    Casta diva, mounts up to show
How high the sky is over harvested Tuscany,
    Over this communist conviviality within the wall
Of a fortress that defends nothing at all.

History turns to statues, to fancy dress
    And the stylishness of Guevara in his bonnet. Here,
Red-bloused, forgetful sales girls
    For the revolution, flirt with the males
At a bookstore under an awning of red:
    Lenin, Che, Debray and Mao—
The unbought titles, pristinely serried.

'Realism and sobriety', one might write of the art show:
    In *No to Repression*, a procession of women
With raised fists, shouts No, No, No.
    And between *American Bombers* and *Black Boy Cleaning Shoes*,
Somebody, unteachably out of step,
    Has gouged intently into paint
The stigmata of St Francis in *Miracle of the Saint*.

Consciences drowse this summer night
    Warmed by the after-glow. Fragrance of cooking
Weighs on the sense already fed by it,
    The wild boar turning and turning on its spit;
And the air too greasily replete to lift the red flag,
    The morning headlines grow fainter in the dusk:
'Where is Dubcek?' 'Tanks on the streets of Prague.'

PARIS IN SIXTY-NINE

for Octavio Paz

'I love', I heard you say,
    'To walk in the morning.' We were walking,
Spring light sharpening each vista,
    Under the symmetrical, freshly-leafing trees,
By boulevard, bridge and quays the Douanier
    Had painted into his golden age
Of a Tour Eiffel perpetually new.
    I replied: 'I trust the thoughts that come to me
When walking. Do you, too, *work* when walking?'
    'Work when I am working . . . ?' My error
(Traffic was too loud to fight with words)
    Came clear to me at last—for I
Am far too fast imagining that my friends
    Prefer, like me, the stir of street or landscape
To four walls to work in. Sunlight
    Had begun, after a night of frost, to warm
The April air to temperate perfection,
    In which the mathematics of sharp shade
Would have gratified Le Nôtre, 'auteur de ce jardin':
    His bust surveyed it: in the pavilion there
The subtler geometries of Cézanne. Refaire
    Poussin après la nature!—he and the auteur
Might have seen eye to eye, perhaps,
    But for the straight lines and the grandeur.
All was not easy here. Gendarmerie
    Clustered at corners, still unrelenting
After the late events, although the theatre
    Deserted by its actors now, lay silent
But for the sloganned walls. 'De Gaulle', I said,
    'Is an unpleasant man.' 'But a great one,'
You replied, to my surprise, for you
    Believed when the students had their Day
It was a sign that linearity
    Was coming to its close, and time
Was circling back to recurrence and fiesta.
    Before the walker the horizon slips from sight.
What matters in the end (it never comes)
    Is what is seen along the way.
Our feet now found confronting us
    The equestrian bulk ('Paris vaut une messe!')

5

Of Henri quatre in the Place Dauphine,
    Horsed on the spot that Breton called
'The sex of Paris', legs of roadways
    Straddling out from it. Was it the image
Drew him to that statue, or had he
    (Eros apart) a taste for monarchy?
'Pope of surrealism' is unfair, no doubt,
    And yet, it comprehends the way he chose
To issue edicts, excommunicate his friends.
    I saw his face look out from yours—
Or so it seemed—the day that I declined
    To dine in company, which led you on to say:
'Always the Englishman, you want to found
    Another church.' So, always the Englishman,
I compromised and came—Paris vaut une messe.
    For it was Paris held us on its palm,
Paris I was refusing as well as you
    And should have said no to neither:
Paris looked in on all we were to say and do,
    And every afternoon concluded with
That secular and urban miracle
    When the lights come on, not one by one,
But all at once, and the idea and actuality
    Of the place imprinted themselves on dusk,
Opening spaces undeclared by day.
    All the recurrences of that constellation
Never reunited us by that river.
    Yet, time finding us once more together
On English soil, has set us talking,
    So let me renew my unrequited question
From twenty years ago: 'Do you, Octavio,
    Work when you are walking . . . ?'

IN A CAMBRIDGE GARDEN

to the same

Another town and time—and little left of it
    Before you were to go. Castles in Spain
Stood solid to receive your royal progress
    While Wren detained us. Beyond his colonnade
Arched and shaded, as if Italian paviours
    Had laid the flags we echoed on—our way
Led us to lawns whose midday shadows
    Seemed cast from trees as massive
I was about to say, as those that grow
    In Mexico itself—but no: this plane,
This copper beech, both take their scale
    From their own setting, and could stand
Nowhere but here, their power contained
    Beside a wall in England. Had you stayed on
Twenty years ago, had I gone
    To live in the house at Nine Mile Swamp,
My children would have been Americans, and you
    An exotic in this Cambridge garden. Now
These inquests on past possibilities
    Serve merely to say that we
Were right to choose the differing parsimonies
    Of the places we belonged to. I thought
That I could teach my countrymen to see
    The changing English light, like water
That drips off a gunwhale driving through the sea,
    Showing the way the whole world
Dipping through space and cloud and sun,
    Surges across the day as it travels on
Turning. In short, I stayed. Your life,
    Pitted against the rigid summa
Of Thomists turned politicians, grew
    More public every year, and mine
In its privacy, more sociable, perhaps,
    Than one that contemplates that upstate view
Over uninhabited acres blank with snow.
    What would you have missed the most?
First, I know, would have come colour.
    We cannot pretend our island exhalations
Do not douse the harshness of that clarity
    That burns back in ochres, oranges and reds

Off Mexican walls. The ground beneath them
　　Wears a brown Franciscan serge—
Not drab, because seen at first intensity
　　Under such a light. Some, I suppose,
—Not you—might find the colours of a place
　　Small reason for living there—
It took an Englishman (John Locke),
　　Meagre and precise, to call them 'secondary'.
And here, fanaticism and moderation meet—
　　I think when Mercader killed Trotsky,
The colours of that garden in Coyoacan
　　Counted for little: he hurried through
Drawn by the thought of what it was he'd do,
　　Senses sheered back to its accomplishment.
So you returned. To the monoxide monotony
　　That taints the trees of Mixcoac—
'There *are* no gardens,' as you said, 'except
　　For those we carry with us.' Now we, too,
Must hurry through the hospitality
　　Of this one, ready for the car
(The gates are opening) that awaits you
　　(And the street looks in.) And so we coincide
Against distance, wind and tide, meet
　　And translate our worlds to one another,
Greet in verse. A poem is itself
　　A sort of garden—we are waving our farewells—
Seasonable at all times as we bring
　　Our changing seasons to it—we are losing sight
Of the speeding car that is launched and one
　　With the traffic now and the mid-May sun.

TÜBINGEN

Today the sun
constructed a sort of ecological clock:
it brings out a shadow
beside each bush—
a dark arrow to indicate
the direction of the flock
that browses the volcanic hill
(it is unsafe for building): up
they climb each morning—
out of the roofs, it seems,
of the surrounding houses.
The shepherd has gone on ahead,
his shadow walking beside him
with his dog. Then one forgets
dog, shepherd and flock
until next morning and the clock
is in motion once more.
But where are the sheep? I see
only shepherd, shadow and dog
striding towards the horizon summit
and the Bismarck Tower that crowns it
bristling with aerials. Dog and man
are like the attendants of some god or goddess—
a suburban Aurora
who has failed to rise. Perhaps the flock
lies nodding beside her. From the street side
none of these hill-top goings on
are visible. *Mensch in Not*
one reads on the beggar's sign:
he is young indeed
for a beggar—there must be more
than meets the eye to this *Man in Need*.
If you sit for long
on the steps of the Stiftskirche
you will be asked
'Do you want drugs?' I ask
myself, 'What is a *Stift*?'—
I must buy a dictionary.
When I return to my rear window
I see with elation
the whole flock up there:

9

the shepherd comes down
to speak to a friend
at the field's edge and the sheep
descend behind him, as if they too
might share in their conversation.
A *Stift* turns out to be
a seminary—there is one here
that Hölderlin attended
who went mad waiting
for the deities of Greece to reappear
on the steps of the Stiftskirche.
I thought of Endymion tonight.
Under a not-quite full moon
the shepherd stood on his hill top
and watched the dog
herd all of his sheep down
in one fleecy sweep.
A bat flickered past.
The sheep continued to flow
then vanish under the roofscape
until the last had disappeared
along with the dog: it is the turn now
of the man to follow
which he does. It was not a bat
but a swallow out late
that dips and returns again and again
in front of a hill where only the moon remains.
I wanted to know
where it was that a flock goes to
regularly at ten o'clock
of a fine June evening, and so
set off uphill one Sunday
(the sheep had failed to appear)
to find what the rooftops were hiding there.
The flock lay huddled together
fenced round by a netted fold
and the dog, now at leisure,
came boldly snuffling up
to the bench I was watching from
and left a wet stain
on its iron leg. A tiny man
with a Punch nose and unshaven chin
a white stubble covered
dismounted from his Honda and began

to collect with care
all the sheeps' dung he could find
as though each piece
were a rare mushroom.
At last Endymion
arrives to inspect the pen.
'You must be content
up here,' I say. Surprised,
'I am more content', he replies
'than I would be down there,
but I am not content.'
The man who grazes and the man
who gazes at him, eye
each other. 'Why are you not content?'
'People dislike sheep. They dislike
the sheep-smell and their dislike—
well, it settles on me. That's why.'
The minute man
with the unshaven chin
has packed the dung
inside an enormous wicker basket
to which he attaches himself, then
mounts his machine
and winds towards the town
with a shut-off engine, as though
he preferred not to break
the silence he is freewheeling through.

BLAUBEUREN

And now the season climbs in conflagration
    Up to the summits. The thick leaves
Glow on either side of the descent
    A fire-ride carves between the trees—
A blue, unsoundable abyss. The sun
    Is pushing upwards, firing into incandescence
Lingering vapours. The tufted pinetips
    Begin to define the hilltop where a cross—
Too blatant to beckon a heart towards it—
    Stands stolid and ghostly, a dogmatic
Concrete post hardening out of mist,
    And, grey to gold, touch by touch,
The wood mass—beams breaking in—
    Visibly looms above the town. Below
Floats back a climbing bell-chime
    Out of the theological centuries: that, too,
Caught up into the burning vibrancy,
    Seems yet another surface for refraction,
Fragmenting into audible tips of flame.
    The beacon of the day—the mist has burned away now—
Blazes towards the death and resurrection
    Of the year. To be outlived by this,
By the recurrences and the generations, as today
    Has lived beyond the century of Dürer—
His rocks stand jutting from the foliage here—
    Is to say: I have lived
Between the red blaze and the white,
    I have taken the sacrament of the leaf
That spells my death, and I have asked to be,
    Breathing it in at every pore of sense,
Servant to all I see riding this wave
    Of fire and air—the circling hawk,
The leaves . . . no, they are butterflies
    That love the ash like leaves and then
Come dancing down from it, all lightness
    And away. Lord, make us light enough
To bear the message of this fine flame
    Rising off rooted things, and render it
Back to the earth beneath them, turning earth
    Itself, while the light still holds,

To a steady burning, a clarity
    Bordering the blue, deep fold of shadow:
Cars, weaving the woodslope road,
    Glitter like needles through the layered leaves.

CAMPOS DE CASTILLA

i.m. Antonio Machado

The storks, back on their bell-towers here,
    Tell winter is at an end. This year
They stayed, but the December sun,
    Flashed off their white, cannot persuade
The months away, stretching between
    The pastel of this frost, its mist of melting,
And the return of green to what appears
    All desert now. The holm oaks
And the vinestocks rear dun presences;
    Fields, fallow to the eye, lie tilled
And quiet above the corn that soon will fill them—
    Soon, that is, in the scope of the wheeling seasons
And of storks, their longevity before them,
    Citadelled on twig-pile summits above Castile.

Alcalá de Henares—Toledo

THE DOOR IN THE WALL

i.m. Jorge Guillén

Under the door in the wall
the slit of sun
pours out at the threshold
such an illumination,

one begins to picture
the garden in there,
making the wrinkled step
seem shadowy, bare;

but within the shadows
an underfoot world puts forth
in points of light
its facets of worth—

surfaces of such depth
you have only to eye them,
to find you are travelling
a constellation by them;

and the sun that whitens
every lightward plane
leaks up the stone jamb,
reappears again

where the flickering tangle
of thick leaves cover
the top of the wall and
ivy piles over.

So the garden in there
cannot mean merely
an ornamental perfection
when the gardener lets be

this climbing parasite
within whose folds
birds find a shelter
against rain and cold.

But let be the garden, too,
as you tread and travel
this broken pathway
where the sun does not dazzle

but claims company with
all these half-hidden things
and raising their gaze
does not ask of them wings—

fissures and grained dirt,
shucked shells and pebble,
a sprinkle of shatterings,
a grist of gravel

where the print and seal
the travelling foot has set
declares, Jorge Guillén,
the integrity of the planet.

AT BOB LUCID'S PLACE

There was enough of summer
in the autumn
to fill the entire afternoon
with sunlit colour,

and there was enough
of silence in the room
to lighten the burden of the city
as it filtered in

through curtains the air kept shifting,
raising among the leaves
of a magazine
tiny tidal sounds

as it breathed them open
and shut them again:
this pulse kept clear
a fluctuating frontier

between the room
and the traffic of feet
and cars negotiating
the intersection on the street

that awaited us,
the shadows of passers-by
advancing eagerly out of a sun
casting them forward from its blaze on the horizon.

AT HANRATTY'S

I catch the flare of fire
at the kitchen door,
out of which emerges
a sweating ballet
of waiters and waitresses.
Do waiters, as Sartre wrote,
act quote waiting unquote? Here,
since half of them
are actors between shows,
the question grows more intricate.
That woman who is acting 'crying'
behind her quivering napkin,
down to the requisite *Boohoo*
(enunciated a little too clearly
to be quite true, however)
lowers her linen guard
to reveal—not the anticipated grin—
but a wet face, and feelings
that are painfully genuine. But do
waiters act? I think Derán does.
She is surprised that I
can recall her unusual name, and so
wants to hear from me what else I know.
She has a way of whirling past
like a small dervish, and indeed,
Turkish by descent, 'my parents'
she explains 'are Kurdies'.
Is this plural all her own,
or an affectionate diminutive
or—she is moving fast—
was it 'Kirghiz' she said?
I ask myself
what Turkish girl would wear
that unkempt head
of electric hair without curl
or unaffectedly try on
such innocent familiarity?
She acts like an American.
That stolid waiter
scarcely acts at all, I think:
we try his patience

by not ordering 'yet', and then
desert his table
(too close to the entrance): he remains
patient and willing
to lend an ear as he passes
to the lady in glasses who
wants to know 'where . . .'—
I cannot hear the rest
and neither can he
but, pivoting on one foot,
bends over closer
to seize her syllables.
Perhaps he, too,—
who knows?—was one of those
who grow into a patience they begin
by merely feigning.
The woman of tears
is leaving, her three
friends steering her by,
supporting her now silent distress
(I glimpse a dry face and eye)
to the door we must follow them through
out and on
into the stir of this street
of nationalities learning parts
that are new to them—of Juans
who would prefer
to be called John.

New York

19

ODE TO SAN FRANCISCO

'I write to you,'
                 he explains,
'in blood,
           four of my friends
having died of late.'
                 He does not state
the cause.
           It is strange
to live in a city where
                 one third of the males
may die of the same malady:
                 an ecclesiastic
of the cathedral is dying:
               what he calls
'a caring relationship'
              has brought him to it.
The writer of travelogues
              is dying:
he continues to speak
             of a tropical infection.
The shape on the side-walk
                 that cannnot sit erect
against the sunlit wall
              but falls forward
is dying—
           the placard beside the begging cup
is there to identify
              the nature of his sickness.
The city
           has an air of medieval fatality.
I once thought it gay
               (that damaged word),
then suddenly
              the bright towers
took on
           a look of such duplicity
I saw that the ocean
              was too weak
ever to cleanse it,
              although the home

of Venus herself—
                        though not of her son Eros.
Hesiod
        calls him the son of Chaos
but that was before
                        succeeding generations
spoke of him
                as that 'mischievous child'
Cupid
        thinking him half a joke.

PORTO VENERE

The older man
is bewitched by the boy
he is travelling with
across the bay:

the boy wears a hat with a brim
as a girl might
coquettishly, and is more
than beautiful to him.

This love has no context
except the day,
the ferry between two ports—
and then?

A walk in the sun
till the next boat comes
to return them where
the far shore glints in the marine sunglare

and the muscular waters
continue to lie—
heaving them to the harbour—
of an inexhaustible physicality

which the severing sea
and the rage of the goddess
who gave her name to this anchorage
keep to themselves forever.

SEPTEMBER SWAMP

The name of the bird that punctuates this swamp
    With its swamp-bird cries
I do not know: that it belongs here
    With that songless song—one
Unhurried, repeated note—is clear
    From the cicadas' dense, unchanging raga,
From the way the water, that scarcely stirs,
    Is seeping invisibly beneath the green
That mantles a slow and certain course
    To the Susquehanna. The leaves that fall
On to this surface will never flow so far:
    All movement is below, save for the blue
Crackle of the dragonflies through static air,
    And turtles like the resurrecting dead, that raise
A serpentine neck and head, and then
    Ease free the whole armoured body,
Sloughing the weed aside, to climb
    A half-sunken log and taste
The luxury of light. They
    Are the consciousness of this place, its satisfaction,
Between the dragonflies' swift, aerial transaction
    And the unsunned fecundity that first gave rise
To swampsong, turtle and to dragonflies;
    That, under the weight of the September heat,
Is urging its furtive current towards open sea.

THE HOUSE ON THE SUSQUEHANNA

A cat stalks by, treading
    From tie to tie of the railroad track
That runs between house and river.
    It is listening to the grass and does not see
The silent immensity of still water
    That flows with no more show of movement
Than the swamps that feed it—yet
    Can take possession of house and town
In one rising sweep. You can tell
    The current by the slight swell at the tips
Of the reflected trees—it scarcely ruffles
    Their riding image. The gleam on the surface
Might almost rekindle that dream
    Of pantistocracy in this spacious place
The dreamers never saw. The house
    On the shore is foursquare and of brick.
In the flailing grass, the cat has its mouse.

*Pantistocracy: this utopian community on the Susquehanna, where all
should rule equally, was the dream of Coleridge and Southey.*

NORTH

It feels like the sea at first.
The raked tails of the planes
resemble the sails of yachts,
and one of these
sticking out from its hangar
is a trapped fish.
AIR NORTH it says
on our fuselage, the stem
on the right hand of the N
sprouting an arrow, and the plane
swings up and out to follow
the sign of that vane, converting
figure to actuality—
up into northair where
below, roads slim, turn
tentative in their approaches
to a landmass they can neither
enfold nor cross: forest:
a lake in the shape
of yet another fish
(how many fish
does that fish hold?)
and the metal of barn roofs,
siloes, sending back
sun-morse, flickering
messages of habitation. Traffic
has thinned on the highways now:
an untidy settlement,
like a thousand, thrown-away
butts of cigarettes, a few,
symmetrical, and the rest
at ugly tangents to one another:
but this fades, too,
into the distances and more
lakes show through the twilight.
The pilot and co-pilot fit
(only a few feet ahead of us)
into a tiny cockpit:
one of them produces and then
spreads wide a map
so that it fills their entire

space: he seems to be checking
points on this
against points on the ground,
but is confused
by the twilight, till he has found
a hand-torch
which he focuses with care
onto the overlapping sheet and (yes)
we are there, almost, and begin
our descent now: down
into Chinese landscapes
of mist and pine, and we try
to read the reality
from the uncertainty of what we see
(is it a snowy contour
or the edges of moving tide
keeps riding in at the spot
where the mountains can hide no longer
the level land?). The wind
that plumps out the air-sock
on the landing field
is the measure of that cold
which strikes through the opening door,
then enfolds us entirely: night
and ahead the unending road,
sharpness of pine-scent, dead
skunk that clings to the tyre-treads
of the waiting car:
it beams us on, into the beginning
of yet more distances until,
downhill out of darkness,
we arrive suddenly at our destination,
drive in among the illumination
of wide-set streets, the town
lights at last of the clapboard north.

GEESE GOING SOUTH

Planing in, on the autumn gusts,
    Fleeing the inclement north, they sound
More like a hunting pack, hound
    Answering hound, than fugitives from the cold:
Flocks, skeining the air-lanes
    In stately buoyancy even seem
To dance, but one's weightless dream
    Of what they feel or are, must yield
The nearer they approach. I sense the weariness
    Of wings that bring them circling down
Onto this cut corn-field
    That offers small sustenance but rest
Among its husks and straw. Rest—
    Yet they continue calling from extended throats
As they did in flight, expending still
    Energies that they will not stint
Crying to one another—is it?—encouragement.
    I break cover for a clearer sight, but they
Instantly perceive this senseless foray
    No hunter would attempt: a thousand birds
At the snap and spread of a great fan,
    A winnowing of wings, rise up
Yelping in unison, weariness turned to power,
    And tower away to a further field
Where others are arriving. I leave them there
    On the high ridge snow will soon possess.
A moon that was rising as the birds came down
    Watches me through the trees. I too descend
Towards the firefly town lights of the valley.
    What does a goose, I ask myself,
Dream of among its kind, or are they all
    Of a single mind where moonlight shows
The flight-lanes they still strain towards
    Even in sleep? . . . In sleep
The town beside these transient neighbours
    Scarcely dreams of their nocturnal presence
Awaiting dawn, the serpentine stirrings
    And restless moon-glossed wings,
Numb at arrival, aching to be gone.

UPSTATE

Climbing across a mountain meadow,
   I was walking—I soon saw—
On no more than a word: 'meadow',
   With all its English aftertaste
Of luscious pasture, of spring flowers,
   Could conceal no longer now
The fact that I was bleeding: barbed stalks
   Had scored my ankles, grasses
Grudged me footroom. I should have come
   Booted and armoured against harm.
At the summit, once thorns had thinned,
   I lay outstretched and submitted to the charm
Of seeing only sky: the golden-rod
   Blotted the distances, thickly nodding
Across my eye-line. Sunbursts:
   And—between—the flickering blade of air
Declared the wind that was tossing the flowers
   And kept the blue so clear today,
Came straight from Canada. You could take
   The measure of arriving autumn here
In the cool, brisk stir that bent
   The woodland larches. Snow
Was invading my mind already as the chill
   Struck into summer. When I came downhill
I took to the wood. It was thicketed.
   Soon, my foot found out what seemed
A wandering border of small stones,
   Their order, or what was left of it,
A human order. Time here
   Rifts as sudden as the weather
In its displacements. They who had ploughed
   Or pastured their beasts where now
Thorn has undone endeavour, lay
   Under this scattering of headstones—some,
As I knelt down, I saw, engraved
   With date and name. History on these hills
Means yesterday, means barns
   And houses that have disappeared already
From the cleared spaces. A graveyard
   In a wood, a brambled meadow—blood
Redefines the word—where growth renews

Between the asphalt highroads and in view
Of the one constant that I hold in common
    With those who died and those who rode away—
The wide circuit of a mountainous horizon.

THE STAIR

The limbs of the giant spruce that leans
    So close to the house, have formed
A kind of stair, a walk-way
    Up to the summit. The squirrel that lives here
Scorns to descend it step by step,
    But with an insane bravado runs
To a branch end, then drops
    Accurately off and, six flights down,
Arrives upright, pine-cone in hand,
    To remain there, tear at and eat it:
Perfectly secure, he is perfectly sane.
    Today, comes snow. We should accept
The long-standing invitation
    To climb those now carpeted treads,
But snow and commonsense say no—
    Such analogues are not to be acted on.
And yet we inhabit our images: squirrel
    Can even seem a god of heights,
The tree his spruce fane. The animal
    Is asleep, and if he were not, he would be
Unconscious of the place devised which we
    Take into our minds and so ascend
The real by way of the imaginary tree:
    Both lean to the house together,
And, even without their deity, can teach
    These wooden walls that this house is a tree house:
We live in a place always just out of reach.

THE TREES

The sunset light is singeing the horizon
　　Above leafless woods, the freeze
Setting its seal on all the tilted
　　Surfaces of the land, on roofs and road,
Till only the trees still stand out there
　　In this after-midnight snow, ledge
On ledge of the pines weighed down,
　　Fingers of fir shaped into distinctness
By the accumulating white. In the dark
　　Of starless dawn, the first plough
Goes through, and early cars
　　Armoured in ice, come crunching out
Over frost, their careful beams
　　Brushing the trunks whose ancestors supplied
These clapboard walls outfacing still
　　Deepening December and the chill to come.

FIRE

'About ship! Sweat in the south . . .'
                Basil Bunting

'It will end in fire,' is what the sun
    Above Mayagüez repeats to the ocean,
And each wave re-tongues it west
    To Cuba and Mexico. The royal palm
Does not hunger and anger for apocalypse,
    But outgrows its own green crown,
Re-tips itself with that lance of green
    That bears a hawk, its beak
As sharp as the point it rides on
    Eyeing back glare. Light,
That is the servant of surfaces, must filter
    To feed its opposite—dark soil
Out of which frangipani and cinnamon
    (Crumple the leaf and you will catch the spice)
And all the growths you cannot name
    Hiding in one another's shade,
Cautiously approach that naked flame.
    But it is westering. The roosting pelican
Sits preening in his tree, prepares
    For the coming cool—foretaste
Of the freshness he must feel tomorrow
    As he dives for fish on fish, and sea
Opens its Eden to him, fire deferred
    In the wide transparency he plummets through.

Puerto Rico

DECEMBER

They are decorating their concrete houses
against the coming season,
the fishermen and the fishermen's families.
Paint-pot in hand, or trailing a festoon
of fairy-lights along the roof,
they pause to say: *Buenas tardes*.
So little space
between them and the hurricane
if it should come this way off the ocean,
except for the single track we have taken.
It divides them from that sea
they cross with so little fear, boat tilted
by the rearward weight
of its outboard, prow
raised above the water
like a horse's neck,
one at the tiller and one
crouched in the scuppers
like the horse's rider.
At the pescadería
they are beaching their craft,
freezing the last of the catch
before the dark comes down.
The fishermen's chapel
has unglazed windows,
and their children, catechized
to the beat of the unbelieving sea,
are watched by the virgin from her boat of flowers,
a sliding pane
drawn between her and them
to keep her from rain and seaspray.
The day's end
stays friendly:
the grizzled fisherman who might almost be
one of the Galileans, asks
where it is we hail from,
and, told, tells us that he
—*o mi padre*—
comes from Corsica. The pelican flock—

33

natives to this place—,
so streamlined in flight,
look drably disreputable,
hunched half asleep already on their nesting tree.

HACIENDA

What I like is when
men take a thing—
this river, say—
and, in the succinctest way,
use and transform it:
at the fall's head here
they have diverted
part of the flow:
a channel now
receives and passes on
through its downhill slot
all of the directed
force that is not
there in untaught nature:
the compacted stream
angles out three ways—one
turns a turbine
to refine the coffee bean;
two flows through
to a grist mill; three
concentrates into
a swirling rush to fill
the open-air Jacuzzi
of planter and family—
then, each rill
released from its man-made
duty shoots out and on
back to its bed
at the foot of the fall,
re-joining itself again to spread
under palm and plantain
across the valley floor,
once more a river.

THE AUTOGRAPH TREE

on whose leaves
you can write your name—
or not, if you prefer
to admire the integrity
of the smooth green skin
that can withstand
salt spray and the Caribbean wind.
Privateers used them
as playing cards,
and the penknife
of the passionate engraver
keeps reminding them
Pedro loves Maria,
the ovate heart
that he incises
echoing the leafshape
at an uncertain angle.
Among flaring neighbours,
rises the flower—
a modestly paper-white affair,
as starkly there as the page
no one has written on.

CROSSING AGUADILLA

Crossing Aguadilla, we get stalled in traffic.
Only patience will see us through: everyone is in town.
How is it these excitable Caribbeans can stay so patient?
Their sense of time must be quite different from our own.
On our way in, the road was already barred
by a procession. A girl with a hard voice
made scratchily severe by amplification, was reading to the walkers
through a microphone passages of scriptural exhortation,
and penitents kept falling on their knees in the dust of the roadway.
Now we are caught between cars, and a blue dragonfly
brightly enamelled as if with car paint
dodges among the scarcely moving cavalcade, and then
floats off to vanish against sea as blue as itself.
Nothing to do but sit here with open windows
that let in the heat and the salsa music,
or roll slowly forward
past the Charismatic Church, the Miracle Pharmacy,
the patch of park where a tiny train
(el tren infantil) with children in it
is going round and round its circular track.
The feather dusters of the sugar-cane blossoms
wave to us from beyond the houses in open country,
but we cannot get there yet out of our half-pleasant purgatory.
We drift in low gear translating the signs—
there is a street here called Absence and another
Happy Days. Next to a McDonald's
large letters say: Jesus is Coming
Prepare yourself. Those for whom these words are meant
continue shopping, as imperturbably intent
as the driver of el tren infantil
that goes on stolidly circling and circling as if for ever.

SAN JUAN

Coming here is like returning to Europe.
The cathedral, marooned among the parked cars,
dates back to Drake who tried
and failed to take the place. Cumberland brought a fleet
and stormed the handsome fort: plague caught him there,
unclosed his grip. Came the Dutch—
these walls withstood them: their masonry is still good.
Down a vista outside of architectural history,
cars file beneath palms to the airport
(the hurricane that leaned on them last week
has left them splayed, or merely brushless broomsticks),
and the ground-crew are standing around our plane,
their shadows projected in front of them
towards this machine that is concentrating their attention.
The flock of egrets beside the runway do not move
as the engines spark into life: they have heard it all before:
if they wished—and they do not—they, too, could be
hanging in the blue above the unseen sharks, or inland,
above roads themselves sinuously in flight
and hardly to be followed out by eye,
hidden by hills as green as England.

FROM GLOUCESTERSHIRE

a letter to Les Murray

I thought of you and of your farm down under—
They were shearing sheep here in the valley field.
Three men. They'd brought their women with them.
The men seemed roughish and the women wild.

I thought of your place once more when I heard them speak.
'Australian?' I said. 'New Zealand,' one replied.
God, how quickly they could strip a sheep
And turn it loose from the fleece it hid inside.

And all sought out their lambs, almost the same
In size, now they had shuffled off that wool,
Stick-legged, kicking jerkily out of it,
Strange in their nakedness, their udders full.

The women folded the fleeces, each as deft
As the sweating shearsmen underneath the trees.
Nuclear Free I read on one of their shirts:
Not joking now, they were civilized in their ease.

At the end of the day one of the men resumed,
'You always get wrong our accents over here.'
'How did you come?' 'Plane to Los Angeles.
Arizona . . . Las Vegas . . . half America.'

Shearsmen and poets travel far these days—
Think of the miles we'd covered when we met
Where dry Judea spreads for the Bedouin
A sparser pasture than our English wet.

The field now is empty of sheep, the migrants gone.
Homebound, they must circle the world again,
Itself a traveller through space and season,
Trailing the wool wisp vapour of their jetplane.

SIGHT AND SOUND

A floating crane
is unloading boulders
from the boat beside it
and transferring them to the tip
of the harbour bar, extending it
in a protective arm far out
into the bay. The crash
of each stone
brings a flash of white
up out of the blue
and a ripple that still has not ceased
to spread before the next
wedding of stone and water
on a risen sea-bed.
The progress—
boulder from boat to sea—
fills a precise three
minutes and then the crane
that has swivelled and swung,
reached into the load and come
back clutching the stone of its choice,
will repeat the arc again
gracefully as before.
Seen from here
the whole operation is silent
(which clearly it cannot be)
and when the load has gone
and both crane and boat set out to sea,
they depart in a majestic, mute cortège
until, suddenly free
of all obstruction
the distance and the air transmit
the engine-beat,
the unhurried pulse of this retreat across the bay,
a single wake cut white behind it.

A GLADE

of hawthorn trees,
                    laid bare
on the seaward side
                    by the constant
flow of sea air,
                clung to the cliff:
on the one hand
                    minute, burnt leaves—
whole leafless branches
                        knotted together
by the grey-green lichen
                        that encased them;
on the other—
                red and flourishing—
berries the birds
                fed from gratefully:
what gave the mind
                    pause in that place
and cause
        to dwell on,
was the way
            the force
of the air had pressed
                        dead boughs
and living into one
                    close intertexture
that roofed in
                a moss-floored room,
a sanctum
            suspended for as long
as the cliff held
                    that was losing ground
already
        to the sea beneath.

THE CHOICE

Between a field of barley and the sea,
Which would you choose to own ten acres of
In substance and in sound? The groundswell pours
Its repetitions in at open doors
Of sense, and shares the threshold with the dry
Sea-whisper of a million beards of barley.
This shimmering estate through which the same
Rumour is running as disturbs the grain,
Dark as the soil and deeper than the roots,
Offers you ownerless rows on rows whose fruits
Are all that happens between sight and sunlight,
Between blue and white. Which will you choose?

ON THE SHANNON

for John Scattergood

Gulls, working their way upstream,
    Turn suddenly dazzling as the sun
Brings the colour of the gorse to life
    On the plain behind them. Here
Where the river loops lazily past
    The walls of Clonmacnóis, two towers
Confront them, from whose crevices
    The nesting jackdaws call, call
Their dark ungainly cries. It is they
    Should be the marauders following the way
The first attackers came and blackened
    The place with fire. That was before
The giant kicked down the castle
    Past whose fragments the gulls fly in,
As white as the spirits of those monks would be
    Risen and returning here to see
Their ruins occupied, hearing beyond these cries
    The silence that first drew them to the spot
Solid throughout the sky, and far below,
    The hardly audible waters still bending by.

IN A CORNISH CHURCH

Lady of alabaster,
you hold in your skirtfolds
your dead children,
and you wait
for that great day
whose explanation
will be clear;
and why so many of you came
only to die here,
leaving no memory
except this unnamed stone
will then appear
perhaps. Till when
you in your whiteness
will abide
as patient as the ammonite
coiled in the cliff,
as if you waited
to reclaim from silence
your living children and your name.

RESPONSE TO HOPKINS

'What by your measure is the heaven of desire . . . ?'

Camomile sweetens the cliff-top grass:
    Below, vivid uncertainties disturb
The massing of these waters: you would not think
    That the tide was receding where they beat,
As the wind piling wave on wave
    Pulls against the insistence of the moon.
And do they belong to the sea or to the sky
    These purples and these greens? The water
Washing its predilections from the eye,
    Carries such light in it, that when the hawks
Red-brown flash by, their colour
    Lightens at the reflection from beneath. Above,
All kinds of cloud—cumulus climbing,
    Fair weather dapple and horizon mist,
Fill up the air-lanes all the way
    Inland to Dartmoor. Their shadows
Move on the waste, hastening across,
    Masking each sunburst and so transform
Space to an inland sea awaiting storm.
    What by my measure is the heaven of desire?
This inconstant constancy—earth, water, fire.

HARTLAND CLIFF

What did we walk into
above that sea?
Our talk persuaded time, perhaps,
that there might be

exceptions to time,
if not to tide
across the bay we lay beside
that dry July.

The oyster-catchers
with raised wings there
balancing on the rocks, ignored
all the airy lures of elsewhere.

And we watched them hover
and poise, sub-theme
and accompaniment
to the waking dream

we had walked into:
I cannot say
whether we stopped the turning world:
time flowing, yet not away,

was at the full along that coast and we
had at our feet
a double sea—
not quite a poem, yet

only the turns of verse
could contain and then let go
the accumulation of that flow
to the shift of light

late afternoon brings
—to the reshaping of the waters
by a moon unseen,
to the sheen and spread of wings.

SONG

To enter the real,
how far
must we feel beyond
the world in which we already are?

It is all here
but we are not. If we could see
and hear only half
the flawed symphony,

we might cease
nervously to infer
the intentions of
an unimaginable author

and stand,
senses and tongues unbound,
in the spaces of that land
our fathers brought us to,

where, what will be well
or not well,
only time
or time's undoing can tell.

SECOND SONG

On each receding bush,
the stipple of snow today
has posted into the distance
this silent company

on the alert for openings
which yesterday were not there,
tracking through field and covert
into the fullness here;

and not on bushes only,
but on stump, root, stone—
why is it a change of weather merely
finds directions where there were none?—

so that each Roman road,
on entering the maze,
crosses the hills in confusion
at the infinity of ways

only a little snow
has chalked in everywhere,
as if a whole landscape might be unrolled
out of the atmosphere.

FEBRUARY

February is the mad month for the fox, the wind
Carries its call now the animal grows blind
With the lust that is hollowing its side,
And darkness darkens the hoarse note of that need.
Daylight comes to our solitary window:
Waking, you see how many creatures go
By night on errands as urgent as those calls,
With all the restless encirclings round our walls
Writ large on the brilliant emptiness out there,
Imprinting the snow of a populous thoroughfare.

THE BROOM

the new wife's tale

I listened hard. I do not believe in ghosts.
    The house was changing. Indeed, I never saw
Such thorough renovation. 'You do not know',
    She said, 'how many ghosts there were
Needed to be laid. The dead
    Don't bury their dead: only the living
Can do that for them—they go on breeding.
    In room after room she multiplied herself
And lay in wait. For him, not me.
    Yet one bright day I entered my own kitchen,
Or almost did—inside the door
    The sight of a broom scratched to and fro.
It was the sound—dry, rasping
    Across the quarries—first made me see it,
Stopped me. It was familiar enough, a stark
    Discordant blue I'd never cared for.
I hurried through expecting the cleaning woman.
    Nobody there, of course . . . It was things
She seemed to cling to—a clock, a chair,
    Now this (it was she had bought it)
Left leaning against the wall, but then I saw—
    Whatever it was she'd meant by it—that I
Must sweep the place clean
    Of all she was re-living or imagining.' Determination
Flawed lines in her young face. I do not believe
    In ghosts, except for the one she saw almost.

ON A PASSAGE FROM HARDY'S *LIFE*

You were a poet who put on the manners of ghosts,
Thinking of life not as passing away but past,
Taking the ghost view of surrounding things,
A spectre who, making his calls in the mornings,
Found satisfaction in his lack of solidity
Before he had entered into true non-entity.
Even in paradise, what you would wish for,
Would be to lie out in the changing weathers here,
And feel them flush through the earth and through you,
Side by side with those you had known, who never quite knew you,
Dreaming a limbo away of loam, of bone,
One Stygian current buoying up gravestone on gravestone.

A NOTE LEFT ON FINDING
TWO PEOPLE ASLEEP

There is a point between our houses where
Comes a sudden lightening of the air
In the dog-days, a breeze that gratefully flows
As an earnest of refreshing company,
When we shall sit beneath your trees and hear
The musical trickle of the stream descend
From pool to pool, imagining the theme,
The 'little phrase' in the sonata of Vinteuil
To have been like that—first stated there
Where the breeze breaks in, to be repeated by
The voices in your sleep, the falling water
And the turning leaves of the long books of July.

BEFORE THE CONCERT

If I could lay hold
on this glass of water and the stable
transparency of its contents
that contain an image of the table

on which it stands—under the glass
a draped, red cloth—
then I should possess not only
that coolness and that red, but both

of the foreshortened lutes
waiting to make music there,
under a curving window
on either side of the reflected score,

but the lutenist
(whose throat is sore today)
lowers a Brobdingnagian hand
and takes away

this universe, and I
watch it wash and disappear
over the threshold of his dryness,
until it's clear—

those minute instruments,
their world quicksilvering into water
under a melting window—
that is a room I shall never enter.

THE PRISONER

This prismatic
green-glass
stopper
of a bottle
long destroyed
stands in the light
from our window where
it has taken up
the grey-white
shell shard
sharing the ledge
beside it: this,
which you might suppose
unchangeable and hard,
it transforms into
the image of a man who
sits there in a hat
—in this vitreous prison
a tight fit—
with one arm
(his left) bent
sideways to accommodate it
better: the top
of the inverted stopper
(now its base)
raises him up
in miniature majesty
on a sort of dais:
the awkward angularity
of the arm and the confinement
of the head confess
such a discomfort
and rigidity, it seems
as if this monarch of littleness
were only waiting
for someone to
remove the shard and thus
permit him to break out of his dream—
and this he does
the instant that I do.

ON A COLLAGE OF
MARIE JOSÉ PAZ

A scrap in this house
of patches, a landscape
photograph opens
a window on a tree. Where

are we? She
has cleared a space
out of elements
neither here nor there.

By the stair of sight,
from the side we cannot see,
I climb down into it,
all at once free

in this tiny confine
I can compare
only to the atmosphere we breathe
in a poem's stanza—

stanza, indeed,
this image that makes room for
entrance, this interior
turned inside out

towards the eye
and the eye's body, the clear
pane of air,
the being here.

ON A GLASS ENGRAVING
BY PETER DAVID

At first sight,
there is nothing to see—
only when he has set
the goblet turning
in its lit cabinet
does the stippled surface
become depth, the image
solidify: his diamond,
among jungle densities
of a summer day,
discovers a tiger,
whose level look
takes us for its prey,
and walls, leaves,
water, all
now burn
from the shadows
above the swirl
of a still, vitreous
whirlpool, where the bowl
arrives at its base and stem:
this glassy water
seems like the pool of origin
at which his dark forms
drink in their light,
but that illumination
flows from the wrist and firm
hand of this zoologist
trained to measure
the minute. His microscope
opens two ways—
the world and the mind's eye
curving together
round this speckled frieze.

PORTRAITS OF HANDS: HALS

Could one guess
the face from the hand?—
this one that grasps, and that
which languishes
lapped in its glove.
It is the well-articulated skeleton
shows in this dandy's
dangling fingers.
An unseen hand
is in hiding
within the snouted crown
of a hat the other hand,
spaced to its swell,
spreads out fingers over. These
old woman's knuckled hands
lie layered
one above the other,
a single finger ringed.
That hand,
about to flow away in paint,
steadies suddenly
grasping the arm of a chair.
The pinch-of-snuff
finger and thumb take hold
of a circular hat-brim.
The hand on hip
of the I beyond all fellowship
beside the clasped
hands of the husband and his bride.
And they accuse this brush
of 'show', but what can they
surmise of a variety whose eyes
deny it daily?

ON A DUTCH PICTURE

This realist knew there are no such clouds
    As those that ply the painted heights
Of his flatland sky. He had seen
    All kinds, no doubt, containing
Every sort of weather, and waiting for a word
    Out of the sea, to say at last
Which of the weathers it was to be.
    He might well have shown the moment
When cloud-bars in evening sky
    Seem to be moveless, were it not
For the still mass of a single tree
    They are drifting towards. But he preferred
To fill his upper air with shapes
    Wholly imaginary, that scale the canvas space
Like his tentative painter's mind
    Finding its way, feeling how far
He has left behind the land down there,
    Hoveringly revealing what is real
In its green extension towards light that catches
    On the steel of sea where it edges against the polder.

THE DISCOVERY

The summer the stream
dried up we tried
following its bed
deep between the high
tree-shut-in banks
almost a tunnel:
no one had walked
that way before
nor could they
now the water reoccupies
the course we clambered:
our cries at finding
stones shaped to our delight
echoed and re-
echoed chambered
in earth and leaves:
if no one
followed us into
the dusty shingle then
we were the first
and last men on the moon

LUNAR

There is no water on the moon, no sound of it:
    Valleys of deafness, giant crania
Split and upended to contain the glare
    Of white-cold light reflected.
Untouchable and untouching, in weighted gear,
    Those who walked here have left behind
The tread of bootprints going nowhere:
    Wind cannot ruffle or weather stain
The flag they planted in this desert whiteness,
    The star-ray that catches the unmoving ensign
Iridescing with the colours of a world away.

THE MORNING MOON

The morning moon
that I failed to see
appeared to stop (you tell me)
above the house-top,

as if it were itself
the sole luminary of day,
shining after frost
out of a cloud-clear sky:

in my picture of the scene
the sun is lost to me,
with this high visitant
in the zenith of the mind's eye.

Mapped, without motion,
so starkly near, so far,
that which I never saw hangs
as still as the pole star.

PICKING MUSHROOMS BY MOONLIGHT

Strange how these tiny moons across the meadows,
Wax with the moon itself out of the shadows.
Harvest is over, yet this scattered crop,
Solidifying moonlight, drop by drop,
Answers to the urging of that O,
And so do we, exclaiming as we go,
With rounded lips translating shape to sound,
At finding so much treasure on the ground
Marked out by light. We stoop and gather there
These lunar fruits of the advancing year:
So late in time, yet timely at this date,
They show what forces linger and outwait
Each change of season, rhyme made visible
And felt on the fingertips at every pull.

OXFORD POETS

Fleur Adcock

Edward Kamau Brathwaite

Joseph Brodsky

Basil Bunting

Daniela Crăsnaru

W. H. Davies

Michael Donaghy

Keith Douglas

D. J. Enright

Roy Fisher

David Gascoyne

Ivor Gurney

David Harsent

Gwen Harwood

Anthony Hecht

Zbigniew Herbert

Thomas Kinsella

Brad Leithauser

Derek Mahon

Jamie McKendrick

James Merrill

Sean O'Brien

Peter Porter

Craig Raine

Henry Reed

Christopher Reid

Stephen Romer

Carole Satyamurti

Peter Scupham

Jo Shapcott

Penelope Shuttle

Anne Stevenson

George Szirtes

Grete Tartler

Edward Thomas

Charles Tomlinson

Chris Wallace-Crabbe

Hugo Williams